Canada Close Up

New Brunswick

David Fancy

Scholastic Canada Ltd.

Toronto New York London Auckland

Mexico City New Delhi Hong Kong Buen

Visual Credits
Cover: Rolf Hicker/AllCanadaPhotos.com; p. I: Barrett & MacKay Photo/AllCanadaPhoto.com;
p. III: Barrett & MacKay Photo/AllCanadaPhoto.com; p. IV: (top left) Robyn Mackenzie/Shutterstock Inc.,
(top right) Stubblefield Photography/Shutterstock Inc.; p. 3: AllCanadaPhotos.com; p. 4: (bottom) Brian
\J. Skerry/National Geographic Stock; p. 5: (top) James P. Blair/National Geographic Stock, (bottom)
Staffan Widstrand/Corbis; p. 6: Rubens Abboud/Alamy; p. 7: FloridaStock/Shutterstock Inc.; p. 8: Daniel
Dempster Photography/Alamy; p. 9: (top right) Robert Estall/Corbis, (bottom right) Mikus, Jo./
Shutterstock Inc., (bottom left) Rolf Hicker Photography/AllCanadaPhotos.com; p. 10: Barrett & MacKay
Photo/AllCanadaPhoto.com; p. 11: Rolf Hicker Photography/AllCanadaPhotos.com; p. 12: Library and
Archives Canada, Acc. No. R9266-318 Peter Winkworth Collection of Canadiana; p. 13 and back cover:
canadabrian/Alamy; p. 14: canadabrian/Alamy; p. 15: (top) North Wind/North Wind Picture Archives,
(bottom) Medical-on-Line/Alamy; p. 17: Library and Archives Canada, Acc. No. 1972-26-768; p. 18: North
Wind/North Wind Picture Archives; p. 19: National Film Board/Library and Archives Canada/PA-048815;
p. 20: Library and Archives Canada, Copyright: Canada Post Corporation; p. 21: Carl & Ann Purcell/
Corbis; p. 22: George F. Simonson/Library and Archives Canada/PA-103066; p. 23: Brian Atkinson/
Alamy; p. 24: The Mariners' Museum/Corbis; p. 25: CP Photo Archives/Chuck Mitchell; p. 26: Michael
S. Yamashita/Corbis; p. 27: (top) James Leynse/Corbis, (bottom) Mike Grandmaison/Corbis; p. 28:
Pictures Canada/First Light; p. 29: Cary Wolinsky/National Geographic Stock; p. 30: (top) canadabrian/
Alamy, (bottom) Wheeler Images/Shutterstock Inc.; p. 31: (left) Kelly MacDonald/Shutterstock Inc., (right)
Melinda Fawver/Shutterstock Inc.; p. 32: canadabrian/Alamy; p. 33: Hulton-Deutsch Collection/Corbis;
p. 35: (top) Photo courtesy of McCain Foods, (bottom) Panosgeorgiou/Shutterstock Inc.; p. 36: Stephanie
Maze/Corbis; p. 37: canadabrian/Alamy; p. 38: (top) National Archives of Canada/C-6718; pp. 38-39:
Barrett & MacKay Photo/AllCanadaPhoto.com; p. 40: (top) Stephen Mcsweeny/Shutterstock Inc.; pp.
40-41: (bottom) Dale Wilson/AllCanadaPhotos.com; p. 41 (top) Repairing a dyke, History Collection,
Nova Scotia Museum, painted by Azor Vienneau; p. 42: Paul A. Souders/Corbis; p. 43: (top) Photo courtesy
of SABIAN Ltd., (bottom) canadabrian/Alamy.

Produced by Plan B Book Packagers
Editorial: Ellen Rodger
Design: Rosie Gowsell-Pattison
Special thanks to consultant and editor Terrance Cox, adjunct professor, Brock University;
Tanya Rutledge; Alexandra Cormier; Jim Chernishenko

Library and Archives Canada Cataloguing in Publication
Fancy, David
New Brunswick / David Fancy.
(Canada close up)
ISBN 978-0-545-98907-7
1. New Brunswick--Juvenile literature.
I. Title. II. Series: Canada close up (Toronto, Ont.)
FC2461.2.F36 2009   j971.5'1   C2009-900238-8

ISBN-10 0-545-98907-8

6 5 4 3 2 1   Printed in Canada   09 10 11 12 13 14

Contents

New Brunswick's official flower is the purple violet.

The black-capped chickadee is the provincial bird.

CANADA

Russia

ARCTIC OCEAN

Greenland (Denmark)

Iceland

Alaska (U.S.A.)

ATLANTIC OCEAN

Yukon

Nunavut

Newfoundland and Labrador

Northwest Territories

PACIFIC OCEAN

British Columbia

Hudson Bay

Alberta

Saskatchewan

Manitoba

James Bay

Quebec

Prince Edward Island

Nova Scotia

Ontario

New Brunswick

Lake Huron

United States

Lake Superior

Lake Ontario

Lake Michigan

Lake Erie

Welcome to New Brunswick!

New Brunswick, on Canada's east coast, is known for its rivers, forests and ocean tides. Called the Gateway to the Maritimes, it is one of the country's smaller provinces.

New Brunswick is Canada's only officially **bilingual** province. One-third of its population of 730,000 is French-speaking. Its history is marked by struggles, wars and **alliances**. For the French-speaking Acadians, New Brunswick is a home to which they returned. Many English-speaking New Brunswickers trace their roots back 200 years to the arrival of the **Loyalists**.

From New Brunswick's past spring different types of music, dancing, food and storytelling. These make the province a rich and exciting place to live, visit or learn about. *Allons-y*!

Chapter 1
Woods and Water

The Bay of Fundy runs along the southeastern side of New Brunswick, dividing it from Nova Scotia. The origin of the word Fundy is uncertain. Some people believe it comes from *fondo*, the Portuguese word for deep. Others say the bay's narrow shape is reflected in the French word for split, *fendu*.

Whatever the source of the name, this 280-kilometre-long, deep bay is called "the world's biggest bathtub" by New Brunswickers. Twice each day, 100 billion tonnes of seawater roll in and out of the Bay of Fundy. When the tides of the Atlantic Ocean push the water to its narrow end, there is no place for the water to go but up, like filling a tub. These are the highest tides in the world, rising in some places to sixteen metres.

The Hopewell Rocks are rock formations that look like giant flowerpots. They were carved over time by the strong tidal waters of the Bay of Fundy.

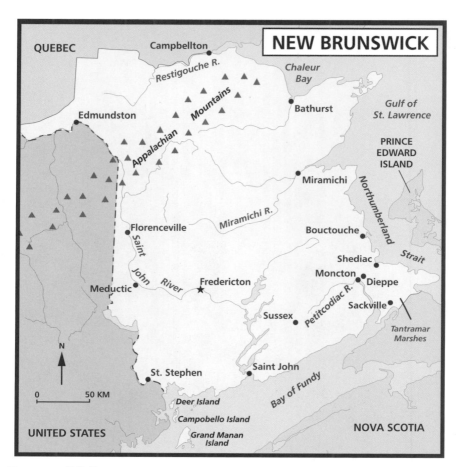

Bay life

Many species of plankton grow in the cold waters of the Bay of Fundy. Fifteen different types of whale come here to feed on them. Sometimes the whales breach, or jump, straight out of the water. Their bellyflop splash landings can be seen from several kilometres away.

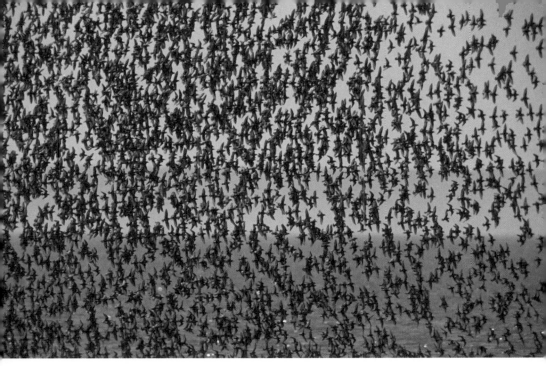
Migrating semipalmated sandpipers fly over the Bay of Fundy, where they feed on the tidal mud flats.

The shore is home to many other animals. About 95 per cent of the world's semipalmated sandpipers depend on the Bay of Fundy mud flats for survival. One hungry sandpiper can gobble up 20,000 tiny mud shrimp in a day. These birds double their weight over a two-week-long feasting period in August. They are then ready for a three-day, non-stop flight to South America for the winter.

A boardwalk curves across *la Dune de Bouctouche*.

Shifting sands

There are many sand dunes along New Brunswick's eastern coast. They form when the roots of plants catch the blowing sand. Constant wind, tides and ocean currents reshape the dunes. Many species of aquatic animals and plant life call the dunes home. *La Dune de Bouctouche* (the Bouctouche Dune) is estimated to be 2000 years old and was created by the carving action of wind after the last ice age.

Sandbars are similar to sand dunes, but are formed in the water by waves and tides. In the province's north, the Eel River rushes into Chaleur Bay and forms the Eel River sandbar – one of the longest sandbars in the world.

The Appalachians

The Appalachian Mountains slant across the northern part of the province, from the United States to Chaleur Bay. They are one of the oldest mountain ranges in Canada. The Appalachians begin in Alabama and end in Newfoundland.

Over 100 species of birds are found in the Appalachian range, including grouse, pileated woodpeckers and grosbeaks. Martens, moose, white-tailed deer and the elusive lynx — a wild cat that is bigger than many dogs — also live in the forests of the range.

Uplands and Lowlands

The New Brunswick Lowlands form the eastern and central regions of the province. The Caledonia Highlands and St. Croix Highlands extend along the Bay of Fundy coastal region. All of these regions are heavily forested with elm, ash, hemlock, silver maple, spruce, larch, birch and jack pine.

Islands in the bay

Grand Manan Island is the largest island in the Bay of Fundy and is part of an archipelago, or group of islands, near the Gulf of Maine. At 18 kilometres wide, the island is small but has an important herring and lobster fishery. Grand Manan also holds the title of "dulse capital of the world" because of the edible seaweed that is collected, packaged and sold here.

Campobello Island, at the entrance to Passamaquoddy Bay, is famous for being the summer home of an American president – Franklin Delano Roosevelt. The home is now part of the Roosevelt Campobello International Park, a park run by both the U.S.A. and Canada.

The Mulholland lighthouse on Campobello Island sits across a narrow strait from Maine, U.S.A.

Farmlands

New Brunswick's major agricultural regions are found along the rivers in the southern part of the province, such as in the Saint John, Kennebecasis and Petitcodiac river valleys. Farmers grow many vegetable crops such as potatoes and carrots in these regions, but blueberries are grown all over the province. The southern part of the province has a warmer climate and a longer growing season, but even here, it's bound to snow by mid-November.

A large potato figure promotes a key crop in New Brunswick.

An edible seaweed called dulse is harvested on Grand Manan Island.

New Brunswick is known for its blueberries, which grow on farms as well as wild in the bush.

9

Cities by the water

Water is life in New Brunswick's communities. Its three biggest cities are located on early trade routes that used waterways for the transportation of timber and furs.

Saint John is on the Bay of Fundy at the mouth of the Saint John River. Fredericton – the province's capital – is divided by the Saint John River, and Moncton is in the Petitcodiac River Valley. Further north, the smaller cities of Bathurst, Campbellton and Miramichi developed next to water too: Chaleur Bay, the Restigouche River and the Miramichi River.

The Saint John River runs through Fredericton.

Natural New Brunswick!

- The world's oldest intact shark fossil – over 400 million years old – was discovered near Atholville in the Appalachian mountain range.

- Old Sow is the largest tidal whirlpool in the western hemisphere. It is in the Bay of Fundy off Deer Island, and is 75 metres across. It got its name from the sucking sound that the water makes as it spins.

- The Saint John River pours as a shallow, narrow waterfall into the Bay of Fundy at low tide. But when the high tides of the bay enter the mouth of the river, the Saint John stops flowing into the bay. The height and volume of the tide actually force the river in the opposite direction, resulting in a reversing falls.

Chapter 2
Hope Restored

New Brunswick's official motto – Hope Restored – was first used by settlers fleeing the American Revolution in the late 1770s. But the province has always been a place of refuge and **restoration**.

The forests and lowlands of New Brunswick were home to the Mi'kmaq and Maliseet peoples for at least 3000 years before the arrival of Europeans. Both groups were often at war with the Mohawk peoples who lived farther to the west. They hunted, fished and grew corn across the region and measured their days in suns and their months in moons.

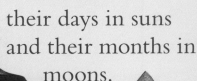

Many place names in New Brunswick – such as Oromocto, Petitcodiac, Quispamsis and Tidnish – are based on Mi'kmaq or Maliseet words.

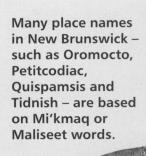

A view of the past

The oldest continuously inhabited village in New Brunswick is located on Metepenagiag Mi'kmaq Nation land. Metepenagiag is the Mi'kmaq name for "the settlement at the head of the tide." The village is located where the branches of the Miramichi River meet, in the northeastern part of the province.

Archaeologists have found that Aboriginal peoples lived and fished for Atlantic salmon, sturgeon and eels here at least 3000 years ago. There are currently over 100 archaeological sites in the area, including digs at ancient villages, campsites and cemeteries.

The Miramichi River at Metepenagiag

Glooscap's warning

Glooscap is the great hero-god of the Mi'kmaq and Maliseet peoples. According to their history, Glooscap told them that people would come to their lands from far across the ocean.

Glooscap's predictions came true in 1534 when French explorer Jacques Cartier's ship crossed the Atlantic Ocean and reached Chaleur Bay. Cartier traded goods with Mi'kmaq in canoes before sailing down the St. Lawrence River.

Jacques Cartier named Chaleur Bay, which means "bay of heat", after reaching it on a hot July day. The deep waters of the bay are usually quite cold.

Samuel de Champlain

In 1603 King Henry IV of France granted Pierre Du Gua de Monts a trading monopoly and named him lieutenant-governor of the French colony of *l'Acadie*, or Acadia. Under his leadership, French explorer Samuel de Champlain established a colony in 1604 on a tiny island at the mouth of the St. Croix River, which today divides New Brunswick and Maine.

The colony was short-lived. The colonists from France – all men – found the climate harsh and cold. They depended on the Aboriginal peoples who lived nearby to help them through the winter. During their first year, 35 of the 79 men died of scurvy, a painful disease that made their hair and teeth fall out.

The next year, the colony was moved to Port Royal where it survived, though de Monts lost his trading monopoly in 1608.

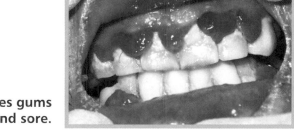

Scurvy makes gums swollen and sore.

Acadian territory

The 1600s and 1700s were a time of **strife** in Europe. France was often at war with Britain and this affected their colonies and territories in North America. Acadia – a French territory that included much of New Brunswick, Nova Scotia and Prince Edward Island – passed back and forth between France and Britain. In 1713 the Treaty of Utrecht, a European war treaty, gave Acadia to the British.

The Acadian residents continued to live peacefully and fish and farm. The British built Fort Lawrence in 1750. The French threatened British territory again in 1751 by building Fort Beauséjour nearby.

In 1755, after a long standoff, 2000 British soldiers from Fort Lawrence attacked Fort Beauséjour, which had just 150 soldiers. The British won the battle. Feeling that the French-speaking Acadians were a threat because they would not swear loyalty to the British crown, they began removing them.

The British read the order to remove the Acadians and set about deporting them.

Le Grand Dérangement tore families apart.

Over 10,000 Acadians were rounded up from all over Acadia and deported in ships to France, Britain and its colonies further south. The waves of deportations, which the Acadians call *le Grand Dérangement*, or the Great Upheaval, lasted until 1762. Thousands of Acadians died at sea, in shipwrecks or from disease while being deported.

Returning home

Following the **Seven Years War** (1756–1763), the Acadians were allowed to return to New Brunswick as long as they took an oath of allegiance to the British.

Over the next twenty years, thousands of people made the trek back to the Saint John River Valley. But the question was: where would the Acadians live? Many new settlers had taken the Acadians' land.

Some Acadians went to northern New Brunswick, while others found their way to the marshlands in Moncton and Memramcook. The descendants of these returning Acadians still live today in the regions resettled by their ancestors.

Many Acadians returned to New Brunswick to build homes and farms where land was still available.

The Loyalists

Many of the English-speaking people of New Brunswick are descended from those loyal to Britain who left the United States during and after the **American Revolution** (1775-1783). These United Empire Loyalists moved north to areas still under the control of the British. An estimated 14,000 Loyalists, including doctors, farmers, labourers and teachers, fled **persecution** and settled along the north shore of the Bay of Fundy. They founded cities and towns such as St. Martins, St. Stephen, St. Andrews and Blacks Harbour.

Loyalists also moved further north to the Chignecto area around Sackville and Dorchester, but the largest number of them – twenty ships worth – arrived in Saint John Harbour in May 1783. The Loyalists spent their first winter in and around the Saint John River Valley, living in tents surrounded by six feet of snow, trying to trap and hunt animals for meat and furs.

The Loyalists endured a harsh first winter in New Brunswick with poor housing and meagre food and supplies.

Actors dress as British soldiers, or "redcoats", in Fredericton during a re-enactment. Loyalists who fought for the British during the American Revolution were given land to settle in New Brunswick.

More refuge seekers

Many others came to New Brunswick during the 1700s and into the 1800s, looking for a better life. Scottish settlers began arriving as early as 1765. Colonists from Yorkshire, England, arrived in the 1770s and 1780s. Waves of immigrants – 80 per cent of them Irish – came to the province between 1815 and 1870, hoping to make a living in the lumber trade.

Confederation

New Brunswick was one of the first four provinces to join **Confederation** in 1867. Politicians in the colonies had been discussing the idea of joining together since the 1820s. They wanted more economic and political independence from Britain. When the Confederation documents were signed, fireworks, **processions**, special prayer sessions and **royal salutes** took place all over New Brunswick.

In June 1877 a giant fire swept through the city of Saint John. Thirteen thousand people were left homeless. The flames jumped from the city to the wooden ships in the harbour, making it look as though the water were on fire.

Changing times

The years following Confederation were marked by deep changes. Machines pulled by horses began replacing the older homemade farming tools. Factories in the cities started making complex metal tools which country blacksmiths could not make. Fishing fleets from other places, with larger boats and better gear, competed with New Brunswick fishermen.

A statue of Sir Samuel Leonard Tilley stands in a Saint John park. Tilley was a New Brunswick politician who supported Confederation and suggested that the country be called a dominion.

New Brunswick shipyards were famous for building wooden schooners and clippers used in the fishing and trading industries.

Cutting trees remained the province's biggest industry, as companies discovered how to make paper out of wood chips instead of from rags. Railways took over from shipping as the best way to bring goods inland. As a result of these and other changes, New Brunswickers started to move out of the province, heading west or to New England for work in larger cities.

Equal opportunities

After Confederation, New Brunswick's economy lagged behind the rest of the country. When it recovered, mills and factories provided employment in the south. But the northern, mostly Acadian areas, were more isolated and lacked the services provided in other areas. In the 1960s, the provincial government passed laws to make things more equal. The government improved health care and education, closing one-room schools and opening new, modern ones.

Premier Louis Robichaud, an Acadian, made New Brunswick bilingual in 1969 – even before the federal government made Canada officially bilingual. This fostered a sense of pride in Acadian culture and encouraged English-speaking New Brunswickers to learn French. A French-language university was opened so that **francophones** would not have to move to Quebec for higher education.

Chapter 3

In Two Languages

New Brunswick is the only Canadian province that is officially bilingual. This means both French and English are used for government services. Many New Brunswickers switch easily from French to English.

Moncton is the most bilingual city in the province. Workers in that city's stores and restaurants jump back and forth between English and French when helping customers. Friends gather in doughnut shops and easily converse in both languages. Sometimes, people telling stories make them a mixture of both languages at the same time!

French spoken here! The colours of the Acadian flag decorate a bed and breakfast for tourists.

Boats line the dock in Chaleur Bay, where fishing is still a way of life.

Bees, frolics and dances

New Brunswick's pioneers did not have much time for fun because they were working very hard to clear land. But they did know how to make their work more enjoyable. People in many early communities would get together for events called frolics or bees.

If someone was putting up a barn, neighbours would come from several kilometres to help chop trees, put up posts and walls, and make food for everyone to eat. These traditions are continued today in community dances, fiddle competitions and events like the Miramichi Folksong Festival, which celebrates the traditional folk music of New Brunswick.

An Acadian fiddler dresses in traditional clothing for a competition.

A massive buckwheat pancake called a *ploye* is cooked at a New Brunswick fair.

La Foire Brayonne, or the Brayon Fair, is held every summer for five days to celebrate the French culture of the Edmundston and Madawaska County area.

Traditional New Brunswick fiddle music mixes influences from many musical heritages in the province, including Irish, Scottish, French, German, English and Acadian. French *violoneux* and English fiddlers play together at parties and festivals.

Another happening special to New Brunswick is *le Party du Parking*, or the parking lot party. At the largest of these, thousands gather in a giant parking lot in downtown Edmundston to enjoy food and music.

Camp time

Although New Brunswickers watch television, listen to and play music, and go to movies like everyone else, their connection to the land is still important. Many families have very simple cottages in the forest called camps. People go to their camps on weekends to relax and to enjoy feasts of corn and lobster. In the fall, these camps are used as a base for hunting deer, bear and moose.

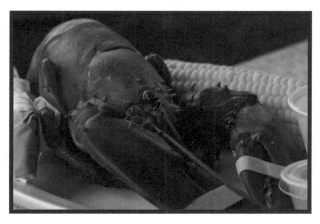

At lobster boils, lobster and corn are cooked together in the same pot.

Fiddleheads and lobster tails

New Brunswickers are fern eaters. Fiddleheads, a type of young fern picked in forests, are a provincial **delicacy**. Served steamed with butter and salt, they taste a bit like asparagus.

Lobster from the Bay of Fundy, salmon from the northern rivers and wild blueberries from cleared forest scrubland are other New Brunswick favourites. Some risk takers will go out on the Fundy mud flats at low tide to pick samphire greens — marsh plants to steam and eat with a garnish of lemon. Pickers must watch the time or they could get caught by the rising tide!

Regional foods are served at *la Foire Brayonne*. *Ploye*, a kind of pancake made with buckwheat flour, is served along with *cretons*, a pork spread. Acadians also claim the invention of *poutine râpée*, balls of grated raw potato and mashed potato filled with salt pork and simmered in water.

Chapter 4
A Resourceful Province

New Brunswick's geography has shaped its economy. The province's abundant forests, mineral deposits, rivers and closeness to the ocean made forestry, mining and fishing its mainstays.

Eighty-five per cent of New Brunswick is covered in forest. These forests have supported many lumberjacks and many lumber and pulp and paper companies over the past 250 years.

Saint John, Nackawic, Miramichi and Edmundston are some of the major centres for pulp and paper mills in New Brunswick today. Here, trucks transport lumber to the mills.

Drivers pull a logjam apart on a New Brunswick river.

There were hundreds of sawmills in New Brunswick in the early 1800s, all located near rivers where the logs were floated and "driven" downriver in the spring, sometimes as giant log rafts. Drivers who rode logs and rafts on the rivers had to be strong and agile, as they could be crushed or drowned by the moving logs.

Logging is still a major industry in New Brunswick and accounts for over 40 per cent of the province's exports. Truckloads of timber arrive at sawmills and pulp and paper mills to be processed into lumber and paper. New Brunswick was the first province in the country to establish forest management plans. Forest management requires replanting and selective cutting so that there will always be trees to cut in the future.

Mineral wealth

When Samuel de Champlain came to New Brunswick, he was looking for copper deposits. Much copper mining activity has occurred since then. One of the world's largest deposits of potash is located near Sussex. It is shipped all over the world, for use in fertilizer, soap and glass. Zinc and lead are also mined in the province's north.

A shipbuilding history

New Brunswick was well-known as a major shipbuilding centre during the age of sail. On one day in the 1850s, 34 ships were under construction in Saint John's 25 shipyards. The shipyards built fast schooners and clipper ships which travelled to China to trade for tea. Merchant and naval ships such as **brigantines** were also made here. Companies competed to build the fastest, biggest and most expensive ships. The wooden shipbuilding industry died out in New Brunswick at the end of the 1800s, when railroads and steel-hulled ships became the preferred way to transport goods.

Dinner is served

Farmers grow potatoes in the rich soils of southern New Brunswick and the Saint John River Valley. McCain Foods, an international frozen foods business, has its roots in the potato fields near Florenceville, New Brunswick. Today the company has factories all over the world, producing a wide range of products including frozen french fries, pizza, appetizers, desserts and juices. The original Florenceville factory is now a 65-million-dollar research and processing plant.

McCain Foods is a family-owned company that opened its first french fry plant in 1957.

The Kennebecasis Valley is known for its cattle farms. Blueberries, some of them wild, and cranberries are grown for sale. Commercial fishers catch crab, lobster and scallops in the waters of the Bay of Fundy, the Northumberland Strait and Chaleur Bay.

The town of Shediac on the Northumberland Strait calls itself the "lobster capital of the world." Fish farming is a major industry off the coasts as well. Here, salmon are grown in large underwater pens. Fly-fishing for salmon in the Miramichi and the Restigouche rivers attracts sport fishers from all over the world.

Workers prepare crab and scallops at a processing plant.

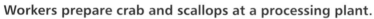

Making connections

New Brunswick is a centre for Internet business and learning. It is now the second-largest employment sector in the province. At any given time, more than 250,000 people from all over the country and around the world are taking an online course over the Internet from a New Brunswick school or company.

An oil and gas empire

New Brunswick has a thriving oil and natural gas industry. Canada's biggest oil refinery is in Saint John. It is owned by Irving Oil, a large oil and gas production and exporting company that began in New Brunswick in the 1920s. Today the family-owned company also has gas stations, truck stops, convenience stores, and transportation and security companies, as well as several newspapers in the province.

Chapter 5
The Tantramar Marshes

The Tantramar Marshes in southeastern New Brunswick are famous for their wild beauty.

The father of Canadian poetry, Charles G.D. Roberts, described them as "Wind-swept all day long, blown by the south-east wind" in his famous poem *Tantramar Revisited*.

Charles G.D. Roberts

"I can see the scattering houses, stained with time, set warm in orchards, meadows, and wheat," he wrote.

The word Tantramar comes from the French word *tintamarre*, meaning great noise or racket. This refers to the calls of the ducks, geese and sandpipers that use the area as a stopover on their migration routes. The marshes have been called the world's largest hayfield because of the high yields of hay grown here.

The soil of Tantramar's salt marshes is high in iodine. This increases the hay's benefit as animal feed.

Tantramar is an area of sea marshes, grasses and low-lying farmland on the southern isthmus of Chignecto – an area that joins New Brunswick with Nova Scotia.

The marshes extend up to ten kilometres inland from the Bay of Fundy. The land was reclaimed from the sea by early Acadian settlers who built a system of **levees** and ditches, with gates to control the water. After a few years of draining seawater and diluting the salty soil with freshwater, the marsh was ready for planting crops.

Migrating mallard ducks are among the thousands of birds that feed and breed in the marshes.

A road runs through the flat wheat fields of Tantramar.

The Acadians were forced to leave these lands during *le Grand Dérangement*. Their property was claimed by Loyalist settlers, as well as by new arrivals from Yorkshire, England. Today the marshes are still farmed and portions are used as bird sanctuaries.

From the 1670s, the Acadians built dikes to turn the Tantramar salt marshes into farmland.

Chapter 6
Points of Pride

▶ Magnetic Hill is one of New Brunswick's most popular tourist attractions. At the bottom of the slope, when you put your car in neutral, it rolls backwards – up the hill! This strange **phenomenon** was first noticed by farmers driving horse-drawn wagons. Scientists later proved that it was an **optical illusion** of the landscape.

▶ The longest covered bridge in the world is in Hartland, New Brunswick. Its 391 metres span the Saint John River. When it first opened more than 100 years ago, the charge was three cents to walk across, and six cents for a horse and wagon.

► Cymbals are an important instrument in orchestras and drum kits. A cymbal company called Sabian was founded in 1981 in Meductic, New Brunswick, and is now famous for making and selling cymbals to musicians all over the world.

► Ganong Brothers is Canada's oldest candy company, founded in St. Stephen in 1873. The Ganongs invented the world's first wrapped chocolate bar in 1910, and were the first in Canada to sell chocolates in a heart-shaped box.

► The University of New Brunswick is the oldest English-language university in Canada. Founded in Fredericton in 1785, the university still uses some of the original buildings.

Glossary

alliances: Unions of groups of people who come together for mutual benefit

American Revolution: A war between Britain and its American colonies (1775-1783) by which the colonies won independence and formed the United States of America

bilingual: Involving two languages

brigantines: Sailing ships with two square-rigged masts

Confederation: The joining of New Brunswick, Nova Scotia, Ontario and Quebec in 1867 to form the Dominion of Canada

delicacy: A special or costly food

francophones: French-speaking people

levees: Embankments, or ridges of earth, built to prevent an area from being flooded

Loyalists: Colonists who supported the British cause during the American Revolution (1775-1783)

optical illusion: Something that appears to resemble something else or to fool the eye

persecution: The ill treatment of people because of their beliefs

phenomenon: Something that can be seen but that causes uncertainty

processions: Groups of people moving forward in an organized way, as in a parade

restoration: The returning of something to its original state

royal salutes: Gun discharges in celebration of royalty

Seven Years War: A European war (1756-63) involving England, France and their allies that spilled over into North America. At the end of the war, France lost its colonies in North America

strife: Stuggle or conflict